The Declaration of Independence

ELAINE LANDAU

Children's Press®
An Imprint of Scholastic Inc.
New York Toronto London Auckland Sydney
Mexico City New Delhi Hong Kong
Danbury, Connecticut

Content Consultant

David R. Smith, PhD

Adjunct Assistant Professor of History

University of Michigan, Ann Arbor, Michigan

Reading Consultant

Cecilia Minden-Cupp, PhD

Early Literacy Consultant and Author

Library of Congress Cataloging-in-Publication Data

Landau, Elaine.
The Declaration of Independence / by Elaine Landau.
    p. cm. — (A true book)
Includes bibliographical references.
Audience: Grades 4–6.
ISBN-13: 978-0-531-12630-1 (lib. bdg.)   978-0-531-14780-1 (pbk.)
ISBN-10: 0-531-12630-7 (lib. bdg.)   0-531-14780-0 (pbk.)
  1. United States. Declaration of Independence—Juvenile literature. 2. United States—
Politics and government—1775–1783—Juvenile literature. 3. United States—History—
Revolution, 1775–1783—Juvenile literature. 4. United States—History—Colonial period,
ca. 1600–1775—Juvenile literature. I. Title.
E221.L36 2008
973.3'13—dc22   2007012254

Find the Truth!

Everything you are about to read is true *except* for one of the sentences on this page.

Which one is **TRUE**?

T or F The tax on tea helped to start the Revolutionary War.

T or F George Washington signed the Declaration of Independence.

Find the answer in this book.

Contents

THE **BIG** TRUTH!

Inside the Declaration of Independence

A mysterious handprint appears on the bottom left corner of the Declaration of Independence.

4 Freedom at Last

Is this why we celebrate the Fourth of July? . . . **37**

New York Harbor was an important port in the
American colonies. Ships carried goods to and from
the busy harbor.

6

CHAPTER 1

A Colonial Beginning

Trading ships from New York Harbor sailed as far as China in the 1700s.

Let's go back in time 250 years. The United States did not yet exist. Instead, there were 13 American **colonies**. The colonies belonged to Great Britain, a country on the other side of the Atlantic Ocean.

Many children in the colonies went to school in a one-room schoolhouse. Students of all ages learned together.

The captain of the *Mayflower* headed for present-day New York, but bad weather forced him to land in Massachusetts.

The *Mayflower* left Plymouth, England, on September 6, 1620. The ship's crew first sighted land that is now part of Massachusetts on November 9, 1620.

People came to America for different reasons. Many **colonists** came because they were not free to worship as they wished in their home countries. Others came hoping to become rich or to seek adventure.

But some people came to America as indentured servants. **Indentured servants** had to work for several years for a master who had paid for their trip to America. Other people came against their will. A large number were taken from their homes in Africa and sold as slaves.

Whatever their reasons for coming, these new Americans were here to stay. By the 1760s, about 1,700,000 people lived in the colonies. They farmed and built towns in what used to be wilderness. They learned how to feed and clothe themselves in this new land.

Native Americans lived in North America long before the colonists arrived. In this drawing, a colonial minister named John Wesley approaches a group of Native Americans in Georgia.

At the time, the government of Great Britain was led by King George III. Britain also had a **parliament** that made laws.

The British government had left the American colonies mostly alone for many years. Colonists picked local leaders, who made new laws. They did not vote for members of the British Parliament. And they paid no taxes to Great Britain.

King George III's rule was the second-longest in British history.

King George III ruled Great Britain for almost 60 years.

Taxes, Taxes, Taxes!

Then things changed. Great Britain fought France in a long, expensive war called the French and Indian War. During the war, the British government borrowed money from British and Dutch bankers to pay for ships, weapons, soldiers, and supplies. The war ended in 1763. Great Britain needed to quickly repay a lot of money. The British government decided the colonies should help pay.

In 1765, Parliament passed the Stamp Act. This law forced the colonists to pay for a government stamp on all paper items. It was like a postage stamp, but it wasn't only for letters. Colonists now had to pay this tax on a newspaper or even a deck of playing cards.

These are a few of the stamps that the Stamp Act required on paper items. The amount of tax that had to be paid varied.

Other taxes came soon after that. Paint, glass, and tea were taxed. The colonists did not produce these goods themselves. They were brought in from another country, or **imported**. When ships carrying goods reached an American port, British officials were there to collect the taxes.

The English colonists were big tea drinkers. So this tax made a lot of people angry.

To meet growing demands, American silversmiths began producing teapots by the beginning of the eighteenth century.

Colonists protested taxes such as the Stamp Act. Here, protesters carry a cloth version of the stamp tax collector on a pole.

The colonists did not just complain about the new taxes. They formed a protest group called the Sons of Liberty. As a form of protest, they **boycotted,** or refused to buy, British goods. The British started losing money instead of making it! Soon King George and Parliament backed down a bit. They removed all the taxes except one—the tea tax. That was Britain's way of showing the colonists who was in charge.

Too Close for Comfort

The British passed a law in 1765 that further upset the colonists. The Quartering Act said that British soldiers could live in colonists' homes. The colonists had to provide the soldiers food and supplies. British officers decided where their men would live. They often chose the nicest homes in town. The colonists were not allowed to say no.

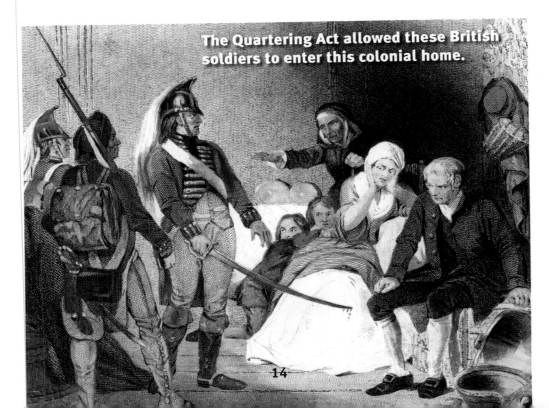

The Quartering Act allowed these British soldiers to enter this colonial home.

The Dutch East India Company brought spices and tea to the world. The company's headquarters in Amsterdam, the Netherlands, is shown here with its warehouses and shipyard.

A Different Cup of Tea

The colonists did not want to pay the tea tax, but they still wanted their tea. They decided to buy it from Dutch **merchants** instead. The Dutch merchants brought tea into the colonies illegally. British tea merchants lost their customers. They were angry!

The British government came up with a plan to get the colonists to buy British tea again. Parliament passed the Tea Act in 1773. This law effectively lowered the price of tea. British tea was now cheaper than Dutch tea. Parliament thought the colonists couldn't resist this bargain. But they could. They didn't want to pay a tea tax, period. It didn't matter how cheap the tea was. They still didn't buy British tea.

The colonists had a good argument for not paying British taxes. They did not elect members of Parliament. There was no one in the British Parliament to speak up for the colonists' rights. So they said Great Britain had no right to tax them. The colonists said it amounted to taxation without representation.

Patrick Henry speaks out against the Stamp Act in 1765, at a meeting of the Virginia government.

Patrick Henry is famous for saying:
"Give me liberty or give me death!"
prior to the Revolutionary War.

Some colonists were also changing the way they thought about themselves. People used to feel they were part of Great Britain. Now some started to think of themselves as "Americans."

Colonists expressed their anger about British taxes by dressing as Native Americans and dumping British tea into the harbor. The next day, people rowed out and sank the tea that was still floating.

CHAPTER 2

Standing Up to the King

Colonists dumped 342 chests of tea into the water during the Boston Tea Party.

The colonists were determined not to pay the tea tax. They knew that standing up to the British government could get dangerous. What if King George III used his military strength to make the colonists obey?

Great Britain was one of the world's most powerful nations in the 1700s. It had a strong military force, including the world's largest navy. British soldiers were already living in the colonies. The colonists believed they would soon need to defend themselves. They decided to form their own military groups, called **militias**.

Many of the men in the colonies joined the militias. There were grandfathers as well as teenagers in these groups. They trained in the fields every evening after work. They did not have fancy uniforms or weapons like the British soldiers had. But they had something important. They believed in what they were doing. They were getting ready to defend their rights.

A Harbor Full of Tea

On December 16, 1773, some Boston colonists showed the British king how strongly they felt about the tea tax and taxes in general. They dressed as Native Americans and rowed out to the tea ships during the night. They were anchored in the harbor. The colonists boarded the ships and dumped every chest of tea overboard. Many people in Boston knew this was going to happen. They lined the docks to watch. This event became known as the Boston Tea Party.

King George III refused to stand for it. He closed Boston's port and ordered the colonists to pay for the tea they destroyed. He sent more troops to the colonies.

The three British East India Company ships that were raided by colonists on the night of the Boston Tea Party were named the *Dartmouth*, the *Eleanor*, and the *Beaver*.

King George III continued to try to make the colonies behave. Parliament passed laws banning public meetings in the colonies, to stop the colonists from planning any more rebellious acts. Then a British general replaced the governor of Massachusetts. The king **appointed** officials who were loyal only to him.

The actions of the British government backfired. The 13 colonies united in support of the people of Boston. They refused to pay the king's taxes. The people of Boston also refused to pay for the tea they had spilled into the harbor.

Colonists Unite!

In September 1774, leaders from all of the colonies except Georgia met in Philadelphia. This monthlong meeting became known as the First Continental Congress. Each colony chose **delegates** to represent them. The delegates wrote an open letter to King George. They said they were still loyal to the king, but they wanted him to respect their rights. King George, however, had other ideas.

The First Continental Congress was held at Carpenter's Hall in Philadelphia. Every colony except Georgia sent delegates.

British soldiers take what they want from a colonial home in this woodcut from the 1700s.

CHAPTER 3

An Important Decision

One nickname the colonists in Boston gave the British soldiers was Lobsterbacks.

The situation in the colonies grew rapidly worse. Colonists wanted the British "redcoats" to leave their homes and towns. Fights broke out between British soldiers and the colonists. Lives were lost on both sides. The **Revolutionary War** had begun.

In Favor of Independence

The colonial leaders knew they had to act. They met again in Philadelphia on May 10, 1775. This meeting was known as the Second Continental Congress.

Sam Adams and John Hancock were delegates from Massachusetts. They had helped plan the Boston Tea Party. They wanted the colonies to declare their independence from Great Britain.

An early battle of the Revolutionary War happened when British soldiers tried to capture Sam Adams.

Sam Adams later became governor of the state of Massachusetts, in 1793.

In the eighteenth century, half of English ships were being used to trade goods like tobacco (shown above) with colonial America.

Another Point of View

Other delegates strongly disagreed. They argued that they were English. Great Britain was their homeland. Many colonists still had relatives there.

Also, they argued that Great Britain was important to the colonists' ability to trade and earn money. Many colonial businesses sold goods to British companies. They made a lot of money from the sales of lumber, tobacco, and other goods.

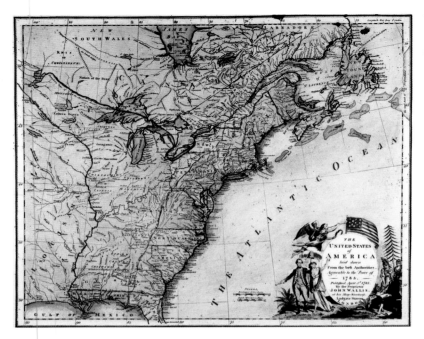

This map shows the United States as of 1783. The thirteen original colonies became the first thirteen states.

Lastly, Great Britain protected the colonies. What if another country attacked? The king had used his powerful army and navy to defend the colonists before. Many colonists did not want to give up this protection.

The delegates at the Second Continental Congress argued for months. They could not afford to make a mistake. The future of every man, woman, and child in the colonies depended on their actions.

At the same time, delegates tried to find a way to win the war. They organized the militias into the Continental Army with George Washington as Commander-in-Chief.

Soon, the Battle of Bunker Hill was fought near Boston on June 17, 1775. The colonists didn't win this battle, but they put up a good fight. The British lost half of their men. This inspired the colonists! They had held their own against one of the world's greatest armies.

The Battle of Bunker Hill pitted 2,400 British soldiers against only 1,500 colonial soldiers.

Meanwhile, some delegates were still trying to work things out with the king. On July 8, 1775, they sent one more letter to King George III asking for fairer treatment. The king refused to even read what they had written.

In this engraving, British Commander Thomas Gage gives children permission to ice skate in Boston, Massachusetts. He orders that any British soldier who attempts to stop the children will be punished.

The Final Step

By May 1776, the Continental Congress had been in session for more than a year. Colonial soldiers had been fighting the British on and off for a year. Colonists had been arguing with the king for more than 10 years. The Americans were ready for freedom.

Thomas Jefferson (right) wrote the Declaration of Independence. Here he shows a draft to Ben Franklin and John Adams.

The Congress chose several men to write another important formal statement, or **declaration**. It would say that the colonies were breaking all ties with Britain.

How would you start a Declaration of Independence? Jefferson's first word was "When."

31

This painting shows Thomas Jefferson, Benjamin Franklin, and other delegates signing the Declaration of Independence.

These men included the outspoken lawyer John Adams of Massachusetts. The well-respected colonial leader Benjamin Franklin of Pennsylvania and Thomas Jefferson were there as well. Jefferson was a 33-year-old lawyer who also owned a **plantation** in Virginia. He did most of the writing. Jefferson proved to be a good choice for this very important task.

Jefferson wrote for 17 days. He wanted the declaration to say what the colonists thought. His writing had to speak for all of them. He created one of the most important documents in world history— the Declaration of Independence.

After Jefferson finished writing, he showed the document to Adams and Franklin. They made some changes, and the three men presented the document to the Continental Congress. On July 2, 1776, the delegates voted for independence. The colonies were on their way to becoming their own country.

The delegates had to be very brave to agree to sign the Declaration. The British saw them as **traitors**. If the British captured them, they would be hanged.

Two signers of the Declaration of Independence later became presidents — John Adams and Thomas Jefferson.

Part 3: Body

"He has refused his Assent to Laws, the most wholesome and necessary for the public good..."

This part of the document lists all the wrongs that Great Britain had done to the colonists. It also explains how the colonists attempted to deal with King George III.

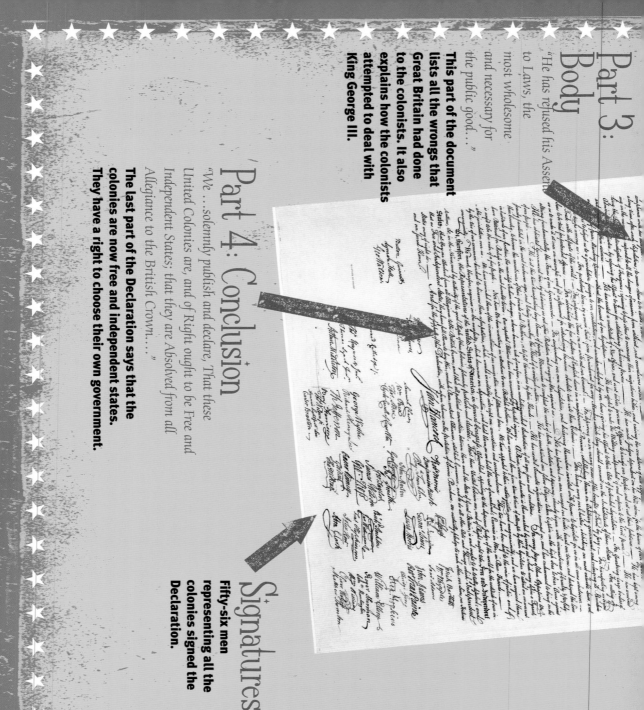

Part 4: Conclusion

"We ...solemnly publish and declare, That these United Colonies are, and of Right ought to be Free and Independent States; that they are Absolved from all Allegiance to the British Crown..."

The last part of the Declaration says that the colonies are now free and independent states. They have a right to choose their own government.

Signatures

Fifty-six men representing all the colonies signed the Declaration.

THE **BIG** TRUTH!

The United States was founded on ideas presented in this powerful document. Here's what you can find there.

Part 1: Introduction

"When in the Course of human events it becomes necessary for one people to dissolve the political bands which have connected them with another..."

This says that if you are going to declare independence, you should explain why.

IN CONGRESS, JULY 4, 1776.

The unanimous Declaration of the thirteen united States of America.

Part 2: Preamble

"We hold these truths to be self-evident, that all men are created equal, that they are endowed by their Creator with certain unalienable Rights, that among these are Life, Liberty and the pursuit of Happiness...."

This is the most famous part of the document. It states that "all men are created equal" and should be given certain rights. These were new ideas at that time!

These are the portraits and signatures of most of the signers of the
Declaration of Independence.

Freedom at Last

George Washington did not sign the Declaration because he was busy leading the Continental Army.

The delegates voted for independence on July 2, 1776. So why don't we celebrate Independence Day on July 2? Because the document was not final yet. The final version was approved by the delegates on July 4 and sent to a printer.

Messengers on horseback swiftly carried printed copies of the Declaration of Independence to all the colonies. Wherever it was read, people cheered and clapped. In many places, bands played and parties were held. Everyone was excited about the future.

The Declaration on the Road

1776

The British threaten to invade Philadelphia. Members of Congress grab the Declaration and flee to Baltimore.

1814

The Declaration is hidden in a Leesburg, Virginia, home during the British attack on Washington, D.C. in the War of 1812.

The first organized Independence Day celebration was held in Philadelphia in 1777. Thirteen rounds were fired from cannons, one for each state in the union.

The first July 4th celebration had fireworks and a parade, much like today.

1941–1944

The Declaration is kept safe in Fort Knox's gold vaults during World War II.

1952–today

The Declaration is on display at the National Archives in Washington, D.C.

Keeping the Declaration Safe

The National Archives in Washington, D.C., has kept the Declaration of Independence safe for more than 50 years. The Declaration was first sealed in a metal and glass case. The case was filled with a gas that kept the document from breaking down over time.

In the 1990s, people noticed that the glass was starting to fall apart. Water from the air could get inside the case and destroy the document.

A new case was built with special metals and painted with actual gold. Today, the restored and protected Declaration is once again on public display.

Visitors view the Declaration in Washington, D.C.

The High Price of Freedom

The colonists soon learned that declaring their freedom was the easy part. They still had to fight for it. The king was not about to let his colonies go. The bloody Revolutionary War continued for the next seven years.

Finally, in 1783, the colonists won with the help of the French. Now the colonies were no longer colonies. They were the United States of America.

Exactly 50 years after the Declaration was approved, two signers — Thomas Jefferson and John Adams — died.

On July 4, 1826, John Adams whispered his last words, "Thomas Jefferson survives." He did not know that Jefferson had died in his home in Virginia just hours before.

41

The colonies were recognized around the world as a new country. Even Great Britain agreed they were now free and independent.

Over time, the country grew bigger and more powerful. Some things never change, though. Americans remain proud of the past. Many are proud of the men who stood up to King George and bravely signed the Declaration of Independence. ★

The Signer Statue stands outside of Independence Hall in Philadelphia. The statue is modeled after George Clymer, a signer of the Declaration.

Writing began on: June 11, 1776

Written by: Thomas Jefferson

Approved by Continental Congress on: July 4, 1776

Number of colonies approving on July 4: 12
(New York approved on July 9th)

Official handwritten document signed on:
August 2, 1776

Size: 29 3/4 by 24 1/2 inches (76 by 62 cm)

Material: A treated animal skin called parchment

Oldest signer: Benjamin Franklin, age 70

Youngest signer: Edward Rutledge, age 26

On display today at: National Archives in
Washington, D.C.

Delivered to the National Archives on:
December 13, 1952

Did you find the truth?

T The tax on tea helped to start the
Revolutionary War.

F George Washington signed the
Declaration of Independence.

Resources

Books

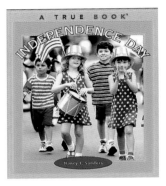

Dolan, Edward F. *The Boston Tea Party.* Tarrytown, NY: Benchmark Books, 2002.

Farshtey, Greg. *The American Revolution.* San Diego: KidHaven, 2003.

Furgang, Kathy. *The Declaration of Independence and Thomas Jefferson of Virginia.* New York: PowerKids Press, 2002.

Hossell, Karen Price. *The Boston Tea Party.* Chicago: Heinemann Library, 2003.

Sanders, Nancy. *Independence Day.* Danbury, CT: Children's Press, 2003.

Stewart, Gail. *People at the Center of the American Revolution.* San Diego: Blackbirch, 2004.

Organizations and Web Sites

Signers of the Declaration of Independence

www.ushistory.org/declaration/signers/index.htm
Check out this Web site for short biographies of each man who signed the Declaration.

Places to Visit

American Independence Museum

One Governors Lane
Exeter, NH 03833
603-772-2622
www.independencemuseum.org
Discover the stories behind America's revolutionary past.

Boston Tea Party Ships & Museum

Congress Street Bridge
Boston, MA 02127
www.bostonteapartyship.com
See the ships used in the Boston Tea Party!

Monticello: The Home of Thomas Jefferson

Thomas Jefferson Foundation
P.O. Box 316
Charlottesville, VA 22902
434-984-9822
www.monticello.org
Tour Thomas Jefferson's house and garden.

U.S. National Archives and Records Administration

700 Pennsylvania Avenue NW
Washington, DC 20408
202-501-5000
www.archives.gov
View the documents that helped shape the United States.

Important Words

appointed – chose someone for a job or an office

boycotted – refused to buy certain goods as a form of protest

colonies – lands settled and ruled by people from another country

colonists – people who live in a newly settled area ruled by another country

declaration – a formal statement

delegates – people chosen to represent others at a meeting

imported – brought in goods from another country

indentured servants – people who worked for several years for a master who had paid for their trip to a new land

merchants – people who sell goods for profit

militias (muh-LISH-uhs) – groups of civilians trained as soldiers, who serve only in emergencies

parliament – a group of people who have been elected to make a country's laws

plantation – a large farm where cash crops are grown

Revolutionary War – a war from 1775 to 1783 that gave the 13 American colonies independence from Great Britain

traitors – people who betray their country

Index

About the Author

Award-winning author Elaine Landau has written more than 300 books for children and young adults. She worked as a newspaper reporter, a children's book editor, and a youth services librarian before becoming a full-time writer.

Ms. Landau lives in Miami, Florida, with her husband and their son, Michael. She enjoys writing about history and often visits the places she writes about. You can visit her at her Web site: www.elainelandau.com.